The magic shoes

Written by Susan Akass

Illustrated by Jan Nesbitt

Heinemann

Prince Ivan was not happy.
He had lots and lots of toys but
he did not like playing with them.
'What can I do today?' he said.

Just then the queen came in and said,
'We are having a dance in the castle.
Go and put on your dancing shoes.'
'Do I have to?' asked Prince Ivan.
'Yes,' said the queen, 'and please be
good because Lord Grump is coming.'

Prince Ivan was cross.
'I don't like Lord Grump,' he said,
'and I don't like dancing.'
But he went to his cupboard to look
for his dancing shoes.

Then he saw a blue bag.

On the bag it said, 'Do not open.'

'What's in here?' said Prince Ivan,

and he put his hand in the bag.

In the bag were some beautiful shoes.

'Here are the shoes for me!' he said,

and he put them on.

But when he put the shoes on,
his feet began to dance!
'Stop feet!' said Prince Ivan,
but the shoes would not stop.
They were magic shoes.

Prince Ivan danced out of his room and over to the stairs. He saw the maid cleaning the stairs.

'Please stop me!' Prince Ivan called, and he put out his hand.

The maid took Prince Ivan's hand but he didn't stop dancing. The magic shoes made the maid dance too! Her bucket fell over and all the water ran down the stairs.

Prince Ivan and the maid danced out into the garden.

'Please stop us,' called the maid to the gardener.

So the gardener took the maid's hand but he couldn't stop them dancing.

The magic shoes made him dance too.

Prince Ivan, the maid and the gardener danced into the kitchen.

'Please stop us!' called the gardener to the cook.

So the cook took the gardener's hand but she couldn't stop them dancing. The magic shoes made her dance too.

Prince Ivan, the maid, the gardener and the cook danced back into the castle. Just then Lord Grump and the queen came into the hall.

'Ivan! What is going on?' said the queen.

‘We can’t stop dancing,’ they all called out.

‘I’ll make you all stop,’ said Lord Grump. He pulled at the cook’s apron but he couldn’t make them stop. The magic shoes made Lord Grump dance too.

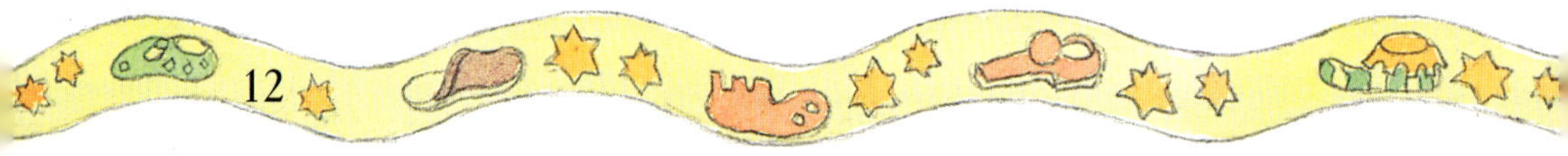

'Do something!' he said to the queen.
But the queen could not catch them.
Faster and faster they all danced.
Then Prince Ivan jumped up into
the air and the magic shoes fell off.

Prince Ivan, the maid, the gardener, the cook and Lord Grump all fell down.

'Oh no!' said Prince Ivan.

'Lord Grump will be very cross now.'

But Lord Grump was not cross. He was laughing. 'Come on,' he said. 'Let's dance some more!'

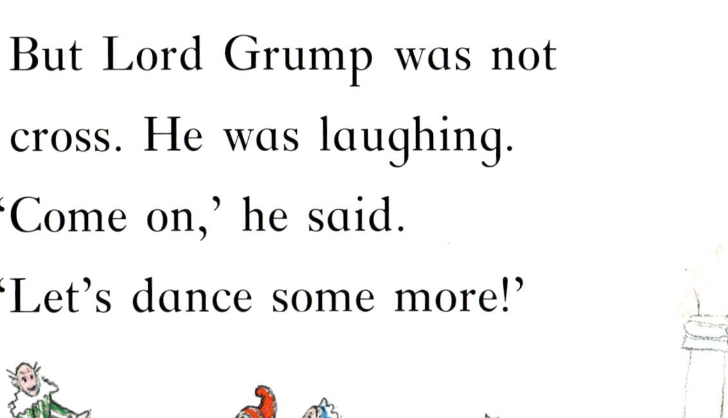

So Prince Ivan, the maid, the gardener, the cook, Lord Grump and the queen danced and danced all day.

When Prince Ivan went to bed he put the magic shoes back in their bag. 'Thank you, magic shoes,' he said, 'but I have danced all I can for one day.'